Hal Leonard Guitar

BLUEGRASS Method

by Will Schmid

MW00669414

CONTENTS

HAL•LEONARD™ CORPORATION

7777 W. BLUEMOUND RD. P.O. BOX 13819 MILWAUKEE, WI 53213

THE AUTHOR

Will Schmid has gained the reputation as an outstanding guitar teacher and performer throughout the United States. He received his BA from Luther College and his PhD from the Eastman School of Music. While teaching at the University of Kansas, he created and performed a series of programs entitled "Folk Music Americana" for National Public Radio. Author of the Hal Leonard Guitar Method, Dr. Schmid has given guitar workshops throughout the United States and Australia. He is currently Associate Professor of Music Education at the University of Wisconsin-Milwaukee and serves on the editorial staff of Hal Leonard Publishing Corporation.

FOREWORD

This bluegrass method book is written for the advanced beginner or intermediate guitar player who wishes to learn basic techniques needed to play the bluegrass style. The book progresses gradually through the skills for playing BACK-UP, BASS RUNS, FILL-IN LICKS and FIDDLE TUNES. Each new technique is provided with practice pieces designed to solidify that skill. The book uses both standard notation and tablature.

PLAYING WITH BANJO

Many of the songs and fiddle tunes in the book are compatible with those found in the HAL LEONARD BANJO METHOD BOOKS 1 and 2. The page numbers for the banjo player are indicated at the bottom of the page on these arrangements. This will allow banjo and guitar players to play together, and it may aid them in forming a band.

ACKNOWLEDGEMENTS

The author wishes to acknowledge the help and support of Charlie Wagner, Robbie Clement, Mike Fox, Mac Robertson and Bob Swan of the Wisconsin Pickin' and Grinnin' Workshops.

HOW TO USE THIS BOOK

Melodies in this book are written in both standard music staff notation and in tablature.

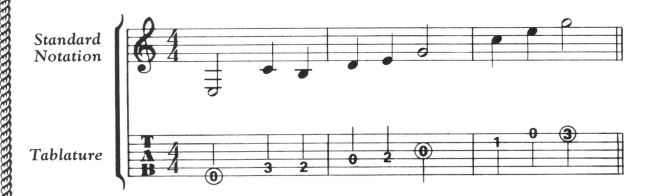

Standard Notation

Tablature

GUITAR TABLATURE GUIDE

Guitar tablature (TAB) is a means of notating finger positions by giving the number of the fret where the finger belongs. The numbers are placed on the line which corresponds to a string on the guitar. If there is an "0", play that string open.

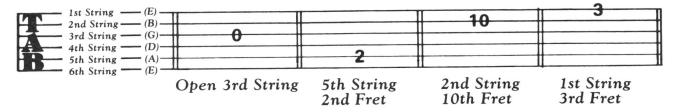

1st String	(E)
2nd String	(B)
3rd String	(G)
4th String	(D)
5th String	(A)
6th String	(E)

Open 3rd String   **5th String 2nd Fret**   **2nd String 10th Fret**   **1st String 3rd Fret**

Time values are the same as those used in standard notation.

| Whole Note and Rest | Half Note and Rest | Quarter Note and Rest | Eighth Notes and Rest | Sixteenth Notes and Rest | Dotted Half Note and Rest | Dotted Quarter Note and Rest |

In a bluegrass band each instrument plays a certain role. The most common role for the guitar is playing **back-up** accompaniment for singing or solos by other instruments such as the fiddle, mandolin or banjo.

The typical back-up pattern is a **bass note** followed by an **afterbeat strum** sometimes known as "boom-chick."

Notice that the bass note is the same letter as the chord name. It is the lowest note or **root** of the chord. The afterbeat strum which follows should be softer than the bass note and should sound strings 1, 2, 3 and perhaps 4. Practice the following exercise until you can accurately pick the bass notes on the correct strings.

PLAYING TIP: Relax and roll the wrist on the afterbeat strum.

Now play the bass note/afterbeat strum as back-up to the "Worried Man Blues."

WORRIED MAN BLUES

See HL Banjo Method Book 1, page 48.

ALTERNATING BASS NOTES

Instead of playing the same bass note twice in one measure, most players alternate between a **primary** and a **secondary** bass note. Below is a chart that shows the string numbers you should pick for most of the common chords:

CHORD NAME	PRIMARY BASS STRING	SECONDARY BASS STRING
A, A7, Am	5	4 or 6
B7	5	4 or 6 (Move 2nd finger to the 6th String, 2nd fret.)
C, C7	5	4 or 6 (Move 3rd finger to the 6th string, 3rd fret.)
D, D7, Dm	4	5 or 3
E, E7, Em	6 or 4 (rare)	5
F (4-string small)	4	5 (Move 3rd finger to the 5th string, 3rd fret.) or 3
F (6-string barre)	6	5
G, G7	6	4

In 4/4 time, primary bass notes are played on beat 1 and secondary bass notes are played on beat 3.

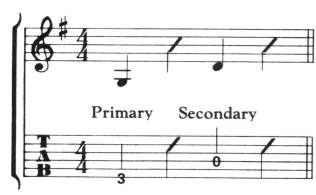

6

The following exercise will give you a good workout on the alternating bass technique for the most common bluegrass chords. The primary and secondary bass string numbers are indicated on beats 1 and 3 of each measure. The slash mark / indicates a strum on beats 2 and 4.

G   **C**

$\frac{4}{4}$ 6 / 4 / | 6 / 4 / | 5 / 6 / | 5 / 4 / |

F   **D**   **G**

4 / 5 / | 4 / 5 / | 6 / 4 / | 6 / 4 / :||

G   **E7**   **A7**

||: 6 / 4 / | 6 / 5 / | 5 / 6 / | 5 / 4 / |

D7   **G**

4 / 3 / | 4 / 5 / | 6 / 4 / | 6 / 4 / :||

G   **B7**   **C**   **G**

||: 6 / 4 / | 5 / 4 / | 5 / 4 / | 6 / 4 / |

                        D   **G**

6 / 4 / | 4 / 5 / | 6 / 4 / | 6 / 4 / :||

When you feel confident of your ability to play the correct bass strings, you can add more interest to your playing by subdividing the afterbeat strums on beats 2 and 4.

⊓ = *down stroke*

∨ = *up stroke*

boom– chick-y -boom -chick-y

Throughout the rest of the book you should feel free to substitute this subdivided strum anytime the tempo of the music is slow enough to permit.

7

Now apply the alternating bass technique to the bluegrass standards, "Hard, Ain't It Hard" and "Sweet Sunny South." The guitar accompaniment is written in tablature on the lower staff.

HARD AIN'T IT HARD

See Banjo Method Book 1, page 39, and Book 2, page 34.

SWEET SUNNY SOUTH

See Banjo Method Book 2, page 46.

2. Take me back to the place where the
   orange trees grow,
   To my plot in the evergreen shade,
   Where the flowers from the river's
   green margin did grow
   And spread their sweet scent through
   the glade.

3. The path to our cottage they say has
   grown green,
   And the place is quite lonely around,
   And I know that the faces and the
   forms I have seen
   Now lie in the dark mossy ground.

BASS RUNS

A bass run is a scalewise pattern of notes that connects the roots (lowest notes) of two chords. The bass run can be used to give your accompaniment variety and to provide momentum toward the new chord. The following section of the book teaches you how to play the principal bass runs and then applies each to bluegrass songs.

G to C Bass Runs

Practice this exercise until the run feels natural under your fingers.

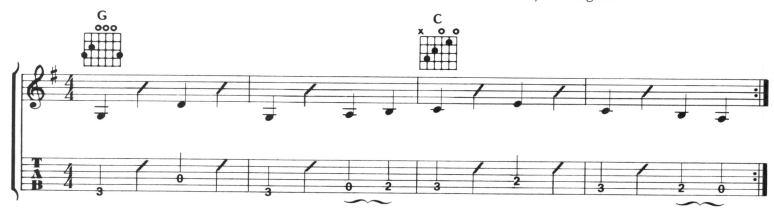

An optional form of the G to C run replaces the 2nd beat strum with another bass note.

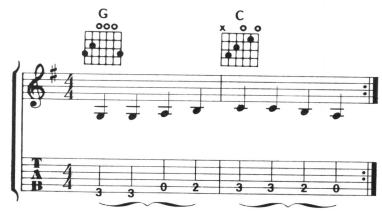

The G to C bass runs are bracketed below the lower accompaniment part. Locate them before playing the piece.

GOIN' DOWN THE ROAD

I'm goin' down the road feel-in' bad Lord,___ Lord, I'm

TAKE OFF CHORD

goin' down the road feel-in' bad. I'm

NO CHORD

goin' down the road feel-in' bad Lord,___ Lord.___ I

ain't gon-na__ be treat-ed this a-way.

See Banjo Method Book 2, page 7.

2. I'm goin' where those chilly winds don't blow (3 times)
   I ain't gonna be treated this a-way.

3. I'm goin' where the water tastes like wine (3 times)
   I ain't gonna be treated this a-way.

JOHN HARDY

See Banjo Method Book 2, page 40.

2. John Hardy went out on the Freestone Bridge,
   Where he thought he'd be free.
   Up stepped the deputy with a gun in his hand,
   Said "Johnny come and go with me."

3. "I been to the East, I been to the West,
   I been this wide world around.
   I been to the river and been baptized,
   So take me to the hangin' ground."

G to D BASS RUNS

Below are exercises which will help you learn the various runs between G and D. First practice the easy runs; then gradually progress through the harder examples.

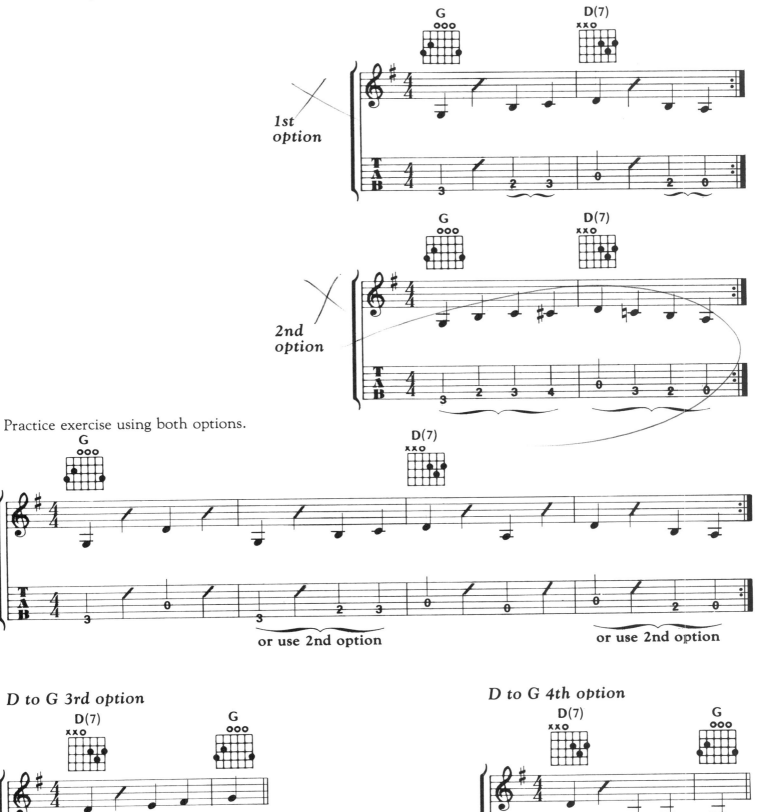

Practice exercise using both options.

Play these new options in measure 4 of the exercise above; then apply them to "My Home's Across The Blue Ridge Mountains" and "Lonesome Valley" on pages 14 and 15.

MY HOME'S ACROSS THE BLUE RIDGE MOUNTAINS

See Banjo Method Book 1, page 47.

LONESOME VALLEY ✗

See Banjo Method Book 2, page 36.

2. Your sister's got to walk that lonesome valley . . .
3. Your brother's got to walk . . .
4. We've all got to walk . . .

CHROMATIC BASS RUNS

You can add extra interest to your bass runs by filling in some of the gaps with notes from the chromatic scale. The chromatic scale uses all of the possible notes, 1/2 step or 1 fret apart, between two points. Following is a chromatic scale between G and C.

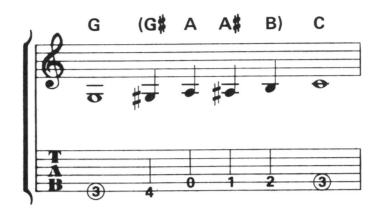

A common $\frac{3}{4}$ run based on this scale is:

Sometimes a chromatic run is made by adding one note as seen in these two examples.

Two of these chromatic runs are used in the next song, "In The Pines" on page 17.

IN THE PINES

See Banjo Method Book 2, page 8.

2. Little girl, little girl, what have I done
That makes you treat me so.
You've caused me to weep, you've caused me to mourn
You've caused me to leave my home.

MORE BASS RUNS

Following are some commonly used bass runs. All examples are written in 4/4 time, but they can be played in 3/4 time by changing the last two quarter notes in each measure to eighth notes.

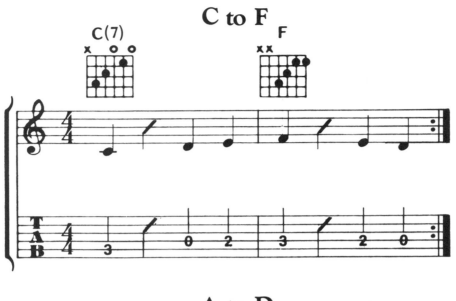

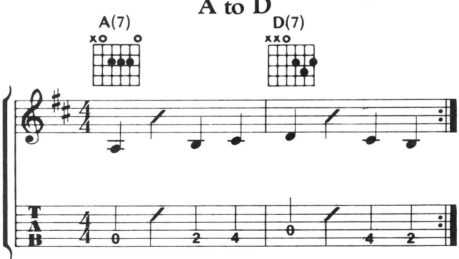

These bass runs usually lead to a minor chord, but a major chord is also possible.

F to Dm

C to Am

G to Em

Once you have developed a solid back-up technique and can effectively use bass runs when needed, you are ready to add fill-in licks. Licks add interest to the bluegrass sound by filling holes in empty sounding measures. These holes are often found at the end of phrases or during long held-out syllables. A caution: Don't hog all of the fills. Other players on banjo, mandolin or fiddle will be competing for the same space.

THE HAMMER-ON

The **hammer-on** is probably the most basic fill. It is played by following these steps:
- Pick an open string (try the 5th) with your right-hand pick.
- Strike the string with the tip of your left-hand finger (try the 2nd on the 2nd fret).

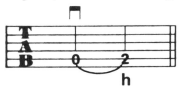

This should feel like you are hammering your finger tip onto a sounding string which then sounds a second higher note. In straight musical terms this is called a **slur**. The hammer-on is indicated by an h below the tablature.

When the hammer-on is put in a 4/4 measure it is usually played as shown in the example at the right.

Try to divide beat 3 into two equal halves. You will find that the hammered-on second eighth note will sound louder and clearer with practice.

The hammer-on for the D chord is given in the example at the right. When you have mastered both the Em and the D hammer-on, play the back-up part to "The Cuckoo".

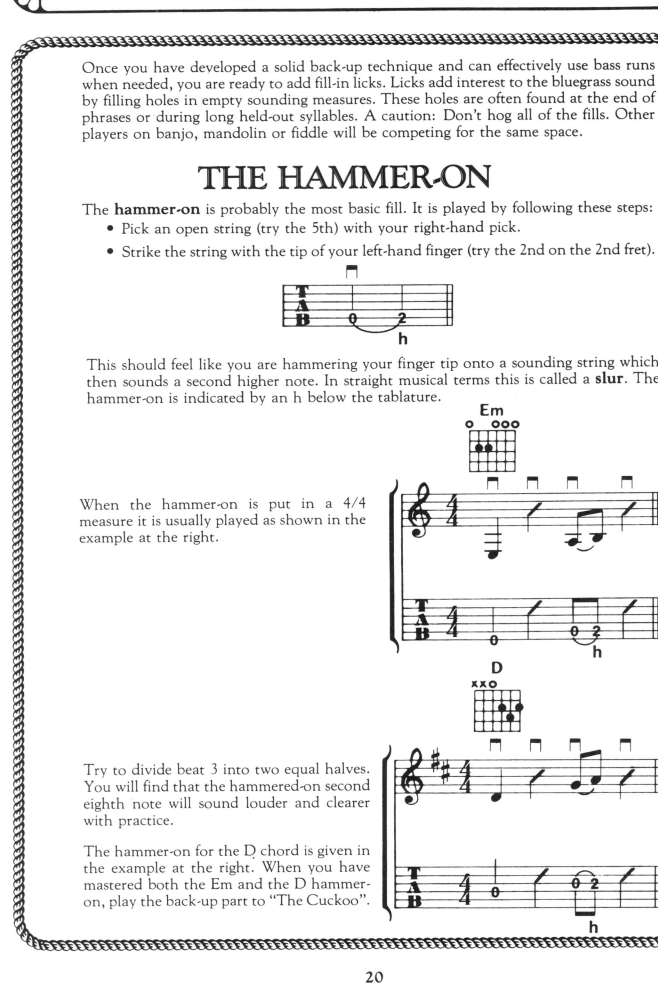

20

THE CUCKOO

See Banjo Method Book 1, page 32.

2. Goin' to build me a cabin on the mountain so high,
   So I can see my true love as she passes by.

3. Jack o' Diamonds, Jack o' Diamonds, I know you of old.
   You robbed my poor pockets of silver and gold.

4. I'm troubled, yes I'm troubled, I'm troubled in my mind.
   If this trouble don't kill me, I'll live a long time.

The hammer-on can be combined with other notes to create many different fills. Study each of the examples below; then work them into some of the songs that follow or some you have already played.

G HAMMER-ON #1

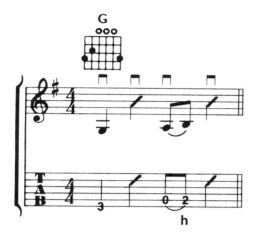

G HAMMER-ON #2

G COMBINATION RUN

C HAMMER-ON

C COMBINATION RUN

22

First learn the song using a straight back-up; then add one lick at a time.

SITTIN' ON TOP OF THE WORLD

'Twas in the spring _____ One sun-ny day

My good gal left ___ me   She's gone a-way

And now she's gone _____ and I don't wor-ry

'Cause I'm sit-tin' on top of the world. _____

See Banjo Method Book 2, page 22.

2. She called me up from down in El Paso,
   Said "Come back, Daddy, I need you so."
   CHORUS

3. Mississippi River runs deep and wide,
   The woman I'm loving is on the other side.
   CHORUS

The pull-off is the musical opposite of the hammer-on. Follow these steps to play the pull-off:

- Pick the string with the right hand while your left-hand finger depresses the string.
- Maintain pressure as you pull the left-hand finger toward the palm of the hand sounding the open string.

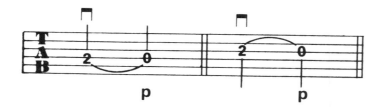

THE G ("FLATT") RUN

The G Run is sometimes called the "Flatt" Run after guitarist Lester Flatt who became identified with it. It can be used within a song and as an ending.

Below are two different ways to play the G Run. The first uses down/up strokes throughout. The second example uses a double hammer-on (two hammers in a row) and a pull-off.

Locate and practice this run in the following songs.

HAND ME DOWN MY WALKING CANE

See Banjo Method Book 1, page 38.

ROLL IN MY SWEET BABY'S ARMS

See Banjo Method Book 1, page 60.

2. Where were you last Saturday night
   While I was locked up in jail?
   Walking the streets with another man
   Wouldn't even go my bail. *Chorus.*

3. I know your parents don't like me
   They turned me away from your door.
   If I had my life to live over
   I wouldn't go there any more. *Chorus.*

4. Mama's a gingerbread baker
   Sister can weave and can spin
   Pa's got an interest in that old cotton mill
   Just watch that money roll in. *Chorus.*

5. Sometimes there's a change in the ocean
   Sometimes there's a change in the sea,
   Sometimes there's a change in my own
     true love
   But there's never a change in me. *Chorus.*

WAY DOWN TOWN

See Banjo Method Book 2, page 38.

2. I wish I was over at my little Rosy's house,
   Sittin' in a big arm chair;
   One arm around this old banjo,
   The other around my dear. CHORUS

3. One old shirt is about all I've got,
   A dollar is what I crave.
   Brought nothin' with me into this old world,
   Ain't gonna take nothin' to my grave. CHORUS

FIDDLE TUNES

Fiddle tunes are a mainstay of the instrumental development of any bluegrass guitar player. Most of these tunes are commonly played on not only fiddles, but on guitars, banjos, mandolins, dulcimers, penny whistles and even on autoharps. They give you an opportunity to practice melodic patterns in a most enjoyable way.

The typical fiddle tune is divided into two parts, each of which may be repeated. All of these tunes are meant to be accompanied by the type of back-up guitar parts you have just learned.

Try some of these ways of practicing the fiddle tunes which follow:

- Tape record a solid back-up guitar part (with runs and licks) at four different speeds, starting slowly and speeding up each time; then play the fiddle tune along with it.
- Find another guitar or banjo player who wants to play duets with you. Trade off playing melody and back-up parts.
- Once you know the tunes by heart, try your own hand at varying the melodies a slight bit. Listen to recordings of these tunes played by good players such as Doc Watson, Clarence White, or Norman Blake.
- Practice carefully. Work toward clarity and perfect coordination of the left-hand fingers and the pick. Keep your pick movement as efficient as possible.

If you play with fiddlers, banjo and mandolin players, you will probably need a capo to accommodate their desire to play in other keys.

- If the fiddle tune is written in G (look at the last chord) and you want to play in A, capo at the 2nd fret.
- If the fiddle tune is written in C and you want to play in D, capo at the 2nd fret.

THE GIRL I LEFT BEHIND

See Banjo Method Book 2, page 23.

THE LITTLE BEGGARMAN
(The Red-Haired Boy)

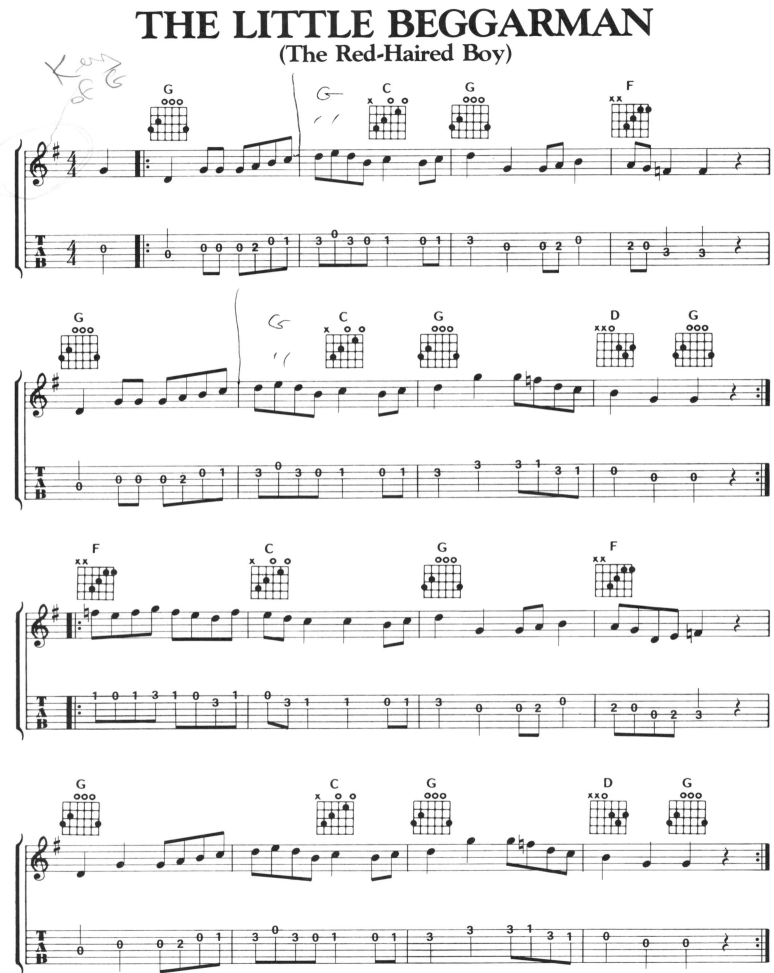

See Banjo Method Book 2, page 58.

MISS McLEOD'S REEL

See Banjo Method Book 2, page 43.

ARKANSAS TRAVELER
(1st Part)

ARKANSAS TRAVELER
(2nd Part)*

*Play as a duet with page 34.

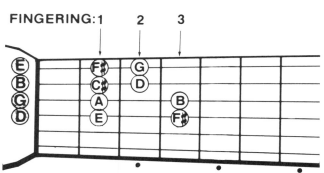

FINGERING: 1 2 3

The "Temperance Reel" is much easier to finger if it is played in 2nd position. 2nd position means that you move your 1st finger to the 2nd fret as shown in the diagram.

TEMPERANCE REEL

(Indicates 2nd position)

(Numbers indicate fingering)

36

THE DEVIL'S DREAM

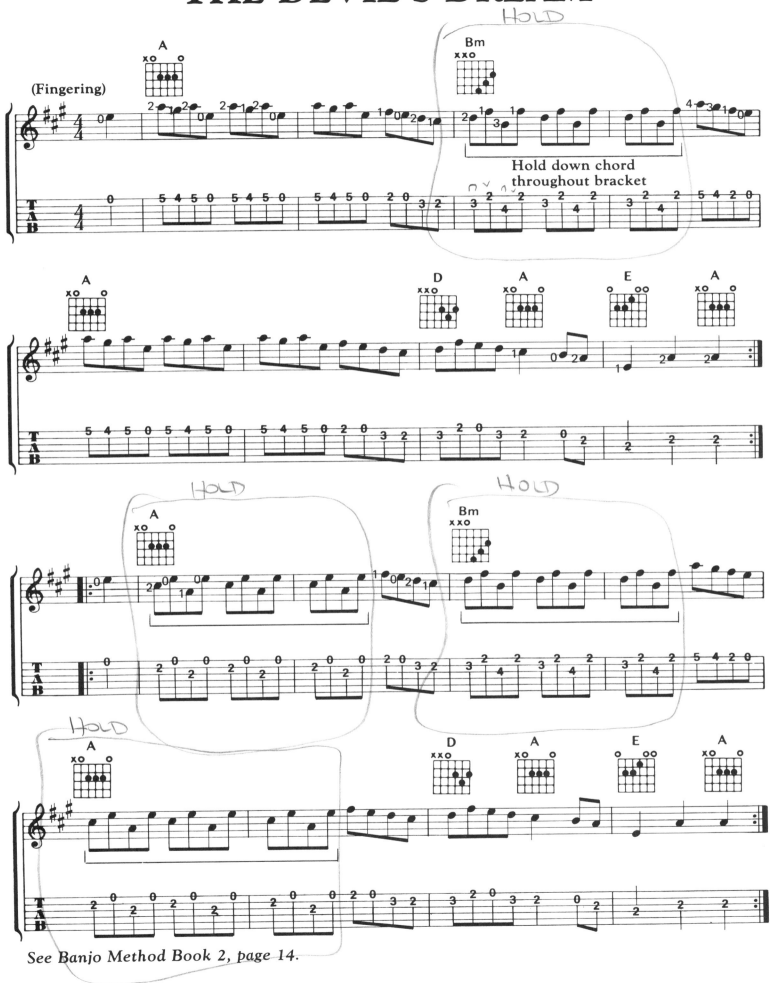

See Banjo Method Book 2, page 14.

BILLY IN THE LOWGROUND
(1st Part)

BILLY IN THE LOWGROUND
(2nd Part)*

*Play as a duet with page 38.

SOLDIER'S JOY

THE SLIDE

The **slide** is accomplished by moving the left-hand fingers along the strings to produce a smear between two notes. To play a slide, follow these steps:

- Depress the string(s) with your left-hand finger(s),
- Pick the string(s) with your right hand,
- Maintain left-hand pressure while your finger(s) slide along the string(s) to a new position.

Try some simple slides between two notes or sliding up to a note:

(Do not pick the second note)

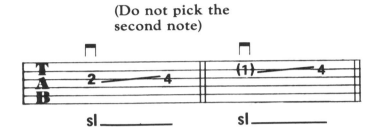

These slides are used on the following fiddle tunes:

"Salt Creek" (p.42)   **"The Eighth Of January" (p.43)**

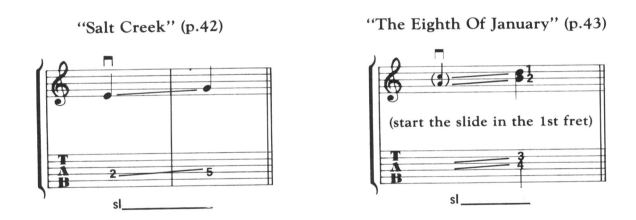

(start the slide in the 1st fret)

"Cripple Creek" (p.44)

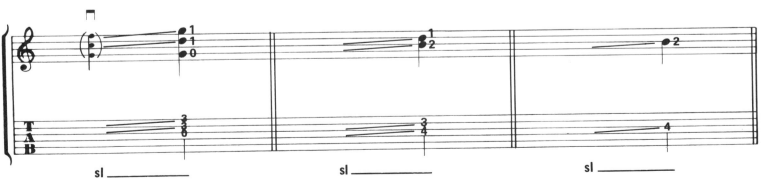

SALT CREEK

THE EIGHTH OF JANUARY

See Banjo Method Book 2, page 42.

CRIPPLE CREEK

See Banjo Method Book 1, page 46.

I gotta gal at the head of the creek,
Go up to see her 'bout the middle of the week.
Kiss her on the mouth just as sweet as any wine,
She wraps her arms around me like a sweet tater vine.

Goin' up Cripple Creek, goin; in a run,
Goin' up Cripple Creek to have a little fun.
Goin' up Cripple Creek, Goin' in a whirl,
Goin' up Cripple Creek to see my girl.

THE SAILOR'S HORNPIPE

See Banjo Method Book 2, page 59.

SCOT'S REEL

Most of "Blackberry Blossom" should be played in 2nd position. (See page 36.)

BLACKBERRY BLOSSOM

THE GUITAR TECHNIQUE SERIES

The books that help you become a better player.

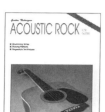

Acoustic Rock For Guitar*

The acoustic guitar has found renewed popularity in contemporary rock. From ballads to metal, you'll find many artists adding that distinctive acoustic sound to their songs. This book demonstrates the elements of good acoustic guitar playing – both pick and fingerstyle – that are used in rock today. Topics include Chords and Variations, Strumming Styles, Picking Patterns, Scales and Runs, and much more.
00699327..$4.95

Basic Blues For Guitar*

This book taps into the history of great blues guitarists like B.B. King and Muddy Waters. It teaches the guitarist blues accompaniments, bar chords and how to improvise leads.
00699008 ....$4.95

Music Theory For Guitar*

Music theory is the cornerstone in understanding music. But how does a guitar player relate it to the guitar? This volume answers that question. Concepts of scale, harmony, chords, intervals and modes are presented in the context of applying them to the guitar. This book will open the door to not only understanding the fundamentals of music, but also the world of playing the guitar with more insight and intelligence.
00699329..$6.95

Finger Picks For Guitar*

A convenient reference to 47 fingerstyle guitar accompaniment patterns for use with all types of music. In standard notation and tablature. Also includes playing tips.

00699125 ....$4.95

Lead Blues Licks*

This book examines a number of blues licks in the styles of such greats as B.B. King, Albert King, Stevie Ray Vaughan, Eric Clapton, Chuck Berry, and more. Varying these licks and combining them with others can improve lead playing and can be used in rock styles as well as blues. Clearly written in notes and tab, you'll progress from the standard blues progression and blues scale to the various techniques of bending, fast pull offs and hammer-ons, double stops, and more.
00699325..$4.95

Lead Rock Licks For Guitar*

Learn the latest hot licks played by today's greatest rock guitar stars, including Jeff Beck, Beck, Neal Schon (of Journey), Andy Summers (Police), and Randy Rhoads (Ozzy Osbourne). The guitarist can use each lick in this book as building material to further create new and more exciting licks of their own.
00699007 ....$4.95

Rhythms For Blues For Guitar*

This book brings to life everything you need to play blue rhythm patterns, in a quick, handy and easy-to-use book. Everything from basic blues progressions to turnarounds, including swing, shuffle, straight eighths rhythms, plus small, altered and sliding chord patterns. All are presented in the style of many of the great blues and rock blues legends. Includes notes and tab.
00699326..$4.95

Right Hand Technique*

Through basic alternate, sweep and cross picking patterns, 10 chord, arpeggios, palm muting and fingerstyle techniques, this book presents everything you need to know in getting started with the basic techniques needed to play every type of music. Additional topics include rhythm, rake and fingerstyle techniques. A real power packed technique book!
00699328..$4.95

Rock Chords For Guitar

Learn to play open-string, heavy metal power chords and bar chords with this book. This book introduces most of the chords needed to play today's rock 'n' roll. There are very clear fingering diagrams and chord frames on the top of each page. Empty staves at the bottom of each page allow the player to draw in his own chord patterns.
00689649 ....$4.95

Rock Scales For Guitar*

This book contains all of the Rock, Blues, and Country scales employed in today's music. It shows the guitarist how scales are constructed and designed, how scales connect and relate to one another, how and where to use the scales they are learning, all of the possible scale forms for each different scale type, how to move each scale to new tonal areas and much, much more.
00699164 ....$4.95

Strums For Guitar*

A handy guide that features 48 guitar strumming patterns for use with all styles of music. Also includes playing tips.
00699135 ....$4.95

* contains tablature